Surround the Job
A Path to Closing Deals

David J. Odess

CONTENTS

Acknowledgements

I want to acknowledge several people who helped me reach this point and showed me that my everyday work – sales – adds value to the companies that have hired me.

My first recognition goes to my father. Although he passed away a few years ago, he remains a great inspiration. He was the "good guy". My father worked hard to make people happy and always looked after their best interests. He taught me to do the same. No matter how hard I've had to work to set up sales, I've always taken care of everyone involved and ensured no one ended up with a one-sided deal.

My business career includes several mentors. Each gave me ways to define success, ones that didn't necessarily focus on a number. Charlie in Cleveland taught me to work really hard and really smart. Ray, Phil, and Alan, in South Florida, showed me the devil is in the details. From Al, a product manager at Westinghouse, I learned the importance of communicating effectively with whomever I dealt with, even if that meant talking in "third grade speech".

I also want to acknowledge Mr. Joel Spira and John Longenderfer. They provided guidance and set me loose to help bring Mr. Spira's desire of a truly international company to life. John, in turn, taught me to look at sales from all sides. He always listened to what I had to say, even if he didn't always agree with my opinion. For that, too, I'm grateful. His viewpoint caused me to think about mine and to decide whether to change or to stick with it.

I can't finish these acknowledgements without mentioning

my family. Sons, thank you for your encouragement. I wouldn't and couldn't have written this book without you. You proved relentless in believing that my career and experiences mean something and should be written down and shared with others.

To my lifelong partner and wife, Holly, Thank You! You didn't flinch once when we went to live overseas. Your adventurous and caring spirit inspire me daily, and you've always stopped me from getting too far ahead of myself. I never worried when I traveled because I knew you were at home managing our lives and raising our three boys. Holly, this book as much yours as it is our sons' and mine.

Purpose

In the beginning of my sales career, I always thought I would sell because there really wasn't anything else I wanted to do that looked like I could earn what I thought was decent money in the early seventies. It paid the bills and selling was a pretty easy job that enabled me to meet a lot of really nice people. There was absolutely no passion in what I did, versus having to have a job and this was a pretty good one and seemed to fulfil my competitive desire. Not competitive with others that sold the same products, versus competitive that I was going to win by closing sales and it felt good.

Over time I realized that I could make really good money and feel good about it and take care of my growing family. And then passion kicked in. What I didn't realize was that I was getting great experience that would help me for many years. I had help from good mentors that honed what I did and I started hearing terms like "straight shooter", "shooting from the hip" and my all-time favorite, "Street Smart". I didn't pay attention to most of this because I was too worried about making a living. When I began to sell in the early seventies, selling was what you did if you didn't have a great college experience or if you couldn't find a job. You never heard someone say, I am going to college to be a salesman or woman. It seemed that you went to college for higher levels of achievement, but not selling stuff.

So, with all that said, back to the purpose of this book. One of the most fulfilling activities I have had throughout my sales career was working with people that were striving to be successful. They are all in a hurry, which helps in sales, and they were smart, observant participants in the sales training and every day activities of selling. Where ever I have been, most sales people want to hear what other sales people are doing to be successful. They want that hidden advantage, whether it is good planning, realizing that good flexible planning does work or just listening to older experienced salespeople that are not condescending or arrogant. I have always enjoyed sharing stories from the road and experiences that I feel can help them become more successful. As most real managers, the more successful my employees were, the more successful I was.

I truly feel that the activity of "Surrounding" a job/project/sale is a successful planned program that will make all salespeople successful. After a lot of encouragement from colleagues and family, I put to paper how and why I did what I did and hope that others will benefit from my experiences and my education on the "street". I have tried to make this as simple as I can to follow and use to be more successful.

I hope you enjoy reading this and hope you gain some new insight on how to be better, more focused and let's not forget, being more "Street Smart" by being more aware of what you are doing.

Good Selling to you all!

Foreword

Dad, I am so excited that you've written this book. Your knowledge and experience are gifts, and I'm glad you're sharing them with everyone else.

With that said, I come into this forward with a bias. I know it. I admit it. But David Odess is my father, so I have the right to be biased, and I unapologetically plan on being so. Numbers, though, do not lie, nor do the people who have worked for and with my father. Just ask them. They'll tell you, without hesitation, that my father is a closer.

There is no better single word that it – closer – to describe what my father does. He closes things. It doesn't matter where and what the sale is or who he's selling to. The sale gets closed.

And when it happens, it's so sweet. He makes it looks easy. But closing doesn't come easy, and it hasn't been easy.

He's hustled all his life. He's had to grind, show grit. And he's had to be a sponge: constantly learning, shifting, adding, changing, and driving his approach. From early days hustling at my grandfather's hardware store to selling commercial lighting in Cleveland, and from working in South Florida to ultimately moving all over the world, he's constantly honed his skills. Things inevitably got in his way. But when they did, he figured out how to get past them and get the sale done.

His life experiences culminate in this book, I'm so excited you've chosen to read it because he has been my biggest secret weapon. I've had the pleasure and honor of watching him at his craft for over 30 years.

It's a gift and I am thankful for it (and for him). A day doesn't go by at work when I don't consciously or subconsciously think, "What would Dad do?" There is no one better at the sales game and no better person to emulate. To me, he is the single greatest sales person who ever lived. I cannot thank him enough for his advice and example, and I am forever grateful for both.

I'm proud, too – proud that he decided to write this book. It's a gift in today's world of ten steps. If you expect to get that here, you bought the wrong book. It's a hard nose, no bullshit guide of what it takes to be the best in sales.

Some of the lessons he's taught me, or I've witnessed are directly or indirectly covered in the coming pages:

1. **Honesty**. This is rule #1. You can do anything to my father, but you don't lie to him. He taught me without trust, the rest doesn't matter.

2. **Hustle.** Being told you won't succeed on a regular basis causes a man to go one of two ways. He either curls up and dies, or he sets out to prove the critics wrong. My father chose the second, using their words to motivate him to win and win and win.

3. **Empathy.** My father always embraced and worked with young or female salespeople when the industry didn't or wouldn't. I saw this softer side of him, and it was awesome. My father fought like hell for his salespeople, and they, in return, fought like hell for him.

4. **Votes.** My father uses the word "votes" to talk about sales. HE always says you can never have

6

too many of them. You have to surround the job and work high and low to capture all the votes.

5. **Confidence.** If you have an opinion, own it. My father trusted his gut, and his gut didn't let him down.

6. **Risk.** My father frequently took calculated opportunities head on. Because of that, we moved a lot. But every step taken was an opportunity to take care of his family and win. Taking it didn't mean he wasn't afraid, but the desire to do better for his family and to win drove him past the fear.

One last thing...I want to share something my father and I haven't discussed in years: the time I almost made the biggest mistake of my life. It's definitely my biggest regret to this day. I was young and dumb and almost didn't take the opportunity to learn from him. I said, "I don't want to follow in your footsteps and get into sales."

What an arrogant, ungrateful, big-mouth I was. I hurt you that day and I haven't forgotten. I hope to make it up to you by continuing to work hard and to be half the father, grandfather, and husband you are.

I'm so happy I had the chance to learn (and still learn) from you.

- Lee Odess, 2018

If money could talk it would tell you that bullshit walks. A simple principal that my mentor, childhood idol, and father, David Odess engrained in me while I developed into a professional. However, it wasn't that only money matter or that it was the only reason to wake up, for my father, it meant far more. My father ensured that I understood that a strong work ethic, absolute focus, and unwavering drive would lead me to achieve my personal and professional goals. Along the way, success would be accompanied by failure, doubt, and at times, sadness. No matter what, I knew I had to rise above it all and push forward, because that's what David Odess, my father, did despite all odds. Life lessons and an uncanny ability to keep it simple made my father successful. An ability to see past the bullshit, to quickly evaluate each situation, unparalleled sales ingenuity, and unmatched ability to build trust with clients ensured that his family had what it needed despite the far off places his job took him. All of this kept him at the top in business and at home. From a simple life to an international businessman, my father has proven that it doesn't take an expensive education or a wall full of awards to be the best. Now, he shares his knowledge, wisdom and experience with the world. I couldn't be more honored to call him, Dad.

- Dan Odess, 2018

Instinct. Innate. Natural. Street smarts. Whatever you want to call it, few have it and most want it. There is something in a few that gives them the ability to know what to say, when to say it, and who to say it to in order to close a sale. When you see someone who has "it", it is a sight to behold. I have luckily had a front row seat to watch one them in action: Dave Odess, my father.

Since I was 13 years old, I have seen my father maneuver around the world, in more countries than I can possibly remember. When people say they sat at the knee of their mentor and soaked in everything they could, I literally sat next to him and watched him conduct business. For most of my life, I never realized what it was that I was watching. I didn't realize how important these lessons were going to be and that they would become the bedrock of my career.

In the first iteration of my career, I thought I was too good to be a salesman. Anyone could do it. I was too smart. I mean, my parents sent me to private schools with the best education money could buy. I was destined for something that actually required skill and education. It took me seven professional years, and a lifetime before, to realize that what my father was and what he did was not only rare, but he was the best at it. Skill, determination, planning, and the thickest skin is required to reach the echelon that my father has reached. In the pages to follow, you will learn, as I did, what it takes to be the best.

The most important thing that I learned from my father is something he never talks about. It is the fact that he worked to live, not live to work. He talks about the fact that "this is not a hobby" and coupled it with the fact that he always brought me and my family along whenever possible. Whether he was eating sushi with one of the leading architects in Japan, seeing behind the scenes of museums in Basque county, or private tours of royal palaces in Europe, he brought us along.

My brothers and I have been bugging my father to write down what he did, how he thought through sales and what made him tick. I was selfish in this request, because I wanted to truly see what it was that made him successful.

9

And I hope that you are able to learn from his experiences as well.

- Todd Odess, 2018

CHAPTER ONE
Sales Serves a Purpose

"When all else fails, go sell something."

The Sales Process as Purpose

I got my first outside sales job through an advert in the local Cleveland newspaper. I headed downtown, filled out an application and waited for a reply. It didn't take long – I had connections to the company, my father had worked for this electrical distributor when I was a kid.

I used to go to work with him and spend hours playing on the company's warehouse floor. Everyone knew me, from my father's coworkers to the owners. (The advice "it's who you know" stood strong then and now. We'll talk more about that idea in the chapter on influencers.)

My father's character worked in my favor. When I applied, I was interviewed on the spot. The sales manager, who remembered my father and his work ethic, said I was hired and ordered me to show up ready to sell the next day.

I didn't know it, but that first job changed my trajectory and initiated a lifelong career in sales. I didn't put much thought into the choice at the time. It was 1974, and I'd left college without a degree. I needed a job and figured I could get one at a company that knew me.

I was right. So, I made good on their decision. I started visiting small electrical contractors and industrial plants to sell the company's products. Something clicked during all those visits, conversations, and negotiations. I realized I had a natural affinity for sales and its process.

I enjoyed strategizing how to surround the job. It was a puzzle. I met with people and listened to them, looked at the pieces of information they provided, and put everything together in order to build my client's confidence in me. The process, not the sale, became my purpose.

I knew how to get the sale. It was a foregone conclusion. I'd done the work to get the sale, so I had nothing to worry about. The sale proved to be relatively anticlimactic at that point. The journey to get there, though, stoked my passion. It still does. It explains why I continue to work in sales and how I've gotten to travel the world selling.

My process works. It has closed sales around the globe, including Shanghai, Dubai, and southern France. It scales according to the customer, too. Thanks to it, I've gotten to work with five-star hotels all along the Vegas Strip, high-end retail companies, oil and gas providers, and global insurance firms, to name a few.

The Assumptive Close

The process worked, but it took me a while to realize that other people in sales could benefit from my experience and expertise. I thought of my process as "street smarts" or "common sense" and assumed people would dismiss it. I didn't have a degree, and I never perused a string of letters after my name. A Harvard graduate surely didn't have anything to learn from me.

Conversations with said graduates and other salespeople have proven to the contrary. They view me as an authority figure in the subject of sales. They see the results and know that my process differs from most of the ones out there, including many of those taught in the classroom or online.

They're right, but it's weird to talk about it. My sons would say it's my humility coming through. I don't know about that, but like I've said before, the process works. If it didn't, people wouldn't request that I share it with their organizations or ask me for advice. I call the process surrounding the job and employ the assumptive close in service of it.

The **assumptive close** is making sure everyone involved (i.e., customers, owners, and anyone holding a vote) assumes you will write the order.

The assumptive close makes the sale a moot point. The sale is the only possible outcome that can occur when a salesperson touches and surrounds all of the influencers by showing and convincing them to use a particular product and company. I successfully used the process to sell electrical components for a small distributor in Ohio as well as high-end electronics with an executive team purchasing for a Monaco high-rise.

The best way I've found to explain the assumptive close is through comparison. A lot of sales books and seminars act like weight-loss commercials. They make grandiose promises and sometimes they deliver. However, the goals remain shortsighted and transient. They concentrate exclusively on a singular element, such as growing leads. They fail as a result.

My process differs. It focuses on principles and processes before delving into specific techniques or components. It might take longer to learn because of that, but it will always deliver real, long-term results.

Surround the job also prevents the whole falling off the wagon. To return to the weight-loss analogy, my system is like choosing to change one's eating and exercise habits rather than investing in some pill or fad diet. A salesperson might make a mistake now and then – and Lord knows I have – but he or she can get up and try again.

Closing Thoughts

I started to explain the process and where I came up with it and it might have caused you to think about whether your sales approach is working for or against you. That's a good thought to have. In fact, I regularly ask it of myself.

Every system, like a classic car, needs checkups and maintenance, particularly as new elements come into play. I started my sales career in 1974. A lot has changed since then. A person can travel anywhere in the world in about a day, we email, we are all online. I have used each of these to enhance my ability to surround the job.

Communication has also undergone a complete transformation. Hardly anybody uses faxes anymore. We live in a digital age. Even though the methods may have changed, the system in this book rarely changed.

The system, remember, encapsulates processes and principles. The technique might change, but the system lasts forever. It's a foundation that will endure and outlast your sales career.

If this chapter seemed a bit heady, don't worry. I'll leave you with two practical tips before we continue onward.

1. If you take nothing else away from this book, take this: **always be surrounding**. Focus on the steps and the assumptive close will follow.
2. Get rid of the busy work. You can fill your days with stakeholder meetings, demos, and presentations. **None of it matter if it doesn't get you to the sale.**

Now that we've set the foundation, let's move onto an aspect critical to setting up the assumptive close: establishing value and gaining consensus.

Exercise 1: Surround the Job

1. Write the name of your project or objective in the center of a piece of paper and draw a circle around it, evenly spaced. This gives 360 degree of points of importance.
2. Make a list of all influencers that will have a vote or influence on whether your product or service will be purchased.
3. Next to each name, put what percentage of the final decision influence they will have, like a pie chart.
4. Place the names around the circle based on the amount of influence you have given to each person. These are dynamic values. Do this monthly or at least after each visit or contact; constantly making sure you are concentrating on each influencer.

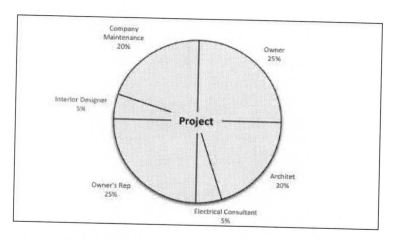

Figure 1. Surround the Job Example

CHAPTER TWO
Establish Your Value

"Your Porsche is someone else's Cadillac."

You know the person: they update to the latest iPhone as soon as it hits the stores or purchase a new car every year. A different person waits until Consumer Reports issues its safety testing reports or receives a sweeter deal on a new phone or table.

Maybe you fall into one of those camps. Perhaps you fall somewhere in between. Regardless, your job as a salesperson is to understand how people view value – no matter how much their outlook varies from yours. Your Porsche is someone else's Cadillac, but both products are automobiles. They get a person from point A to point B.

But while the product remains the same, the value for it varies from person to person. You need to research to discover what value means to the individuals and establish it according to their perspectives. When you do, you'll achieve something remarkable: consensus. Everyone in the room agrees that your offering, be it a product or service, holds value to them. Thus, they agree to the purchase, and you close the sale.

Different Customers, Different Values

You typically see two types of value: **short-term** and **long-term**. You might not know which one your stakeholder prefers, but you can figure out through conversations and research You should seek that understanding because it grants the ability to speak with people in their language. If you understand where they're coming from and how they determine value, you can offer benefits and outcomes that matter most to them.

Cross-cultural Example. When I travel to Hong Kong, I check my assumptions. East Asian people root their decisions in a completely different worldview than mine. If I ignore that difference, I'll never surround the job. I'll bumble through meetings and never get asked to the negotiating table.

If, however, I listen to the people I'm meeting with, study their cultural history and learn their social cues and mores, I can communicate coherently and effectively about value. I recognize what matters to them and respond appropriately.

As a result, I not only close more sales but also build relationships. They trust me because I listen to them, respect their values, deliver the details needed to make an informed purchasing decision, and share information that can be easily communicated to their employees, managers, and owners.

Don't miss the importance of determining value. It's pivotal to getting the assumptive close and surround the job.

19

When you encircle a person with their valued touch points, they inevitably agree that your product is the best product.

Short-Term Value

It's tempting to think of short-term value as some sort of bad guy, but it isn't inherently evil. Short-term value, particularly in relation to financial matters, holds great importance.

Short-term occurs in or relating to a relatively short period of time.

You need people who think short-term. They see immediate impacts, which their long-term peers could miss. The latter get so caught up in the big picture that they lose sight of daily workflows and operational needs.

Because of that, you need stakeholders who care about the short-term. They recognize how a new product will affect employees and clients. They also might raise concerns that need to be addressed prior to rolling out a new product or service.

In the commercial lighting world, short-term investments usually arise with subcontractors or people in mid-management roles. A subcontractor on a construction project usually picks a product, if more than one is named equal, for three reasons.

1. Cheapest price
2. Good, past experience with the product
3. Good relationship with the person selling the product

Establishing short-term value with the subcontractor is

easy. A reliable product at the right price holds maximum value for this person. But if you neglect the subcontractor's concerns and instead focus on longevity or futureproofing, you'll lose the sale. You have to surround the subcontractor with what he or she values most to gain the assumptive close.

Once you realize how the customer orients toward value, you can shift the conversation. You might even be able to address potential roadblocks before the customer gives voice to them. In doing so, you become indispensable because you understand their position, as well as their expectations.

Long-Term Value

Long-term thinkers are needed, too. They care about sustainable value creation, not immediate and sometimes temporary effects. They want to know that your product will deliver a return months and years from now.

Long-term value occurs over or relating to a relative long period of time.

To convince the long-term folks, you will again need to see things from their perspective. They want to know about high-level impacts and future projects. They more than likely will desire information about cost savings, efficiency, and profits, too.

In the commercial lighting example above, the subcontractor cares about price – short-term value. An owner or upper management, though, value long-term results. He or she reviews every large product purchase and tells contractors what to buy.

21

The owner seeks quality products with long-term warranties to protect the lift of a building or other investment. He or she will also pursue companies with reputations for best-in-class customer service and satisfaction.

To surround the owner, you must speak to lifetime value. You must also showcase winning customer service and provide information about your company, such as reviews and recommendations. The owner finds value in quality service and products, not price.

If you can provide data and speak a long-term person's language, you will win that person to your cause. He or she feels understood, and let's be real here...numbers matter, but people's emotions and relationships often matter more. By meeting a person's emotional and logical needs, you will become the go-to resource for a particular product or service.

Your Value

As we have seen, different stakeholders hold different values. You get it. But think about this one. Do stakeholders view you as valuable?

A **value proposition** is a positioning statement that explains what benefits you provide for whom and how you differ from the competition.

Usually, value propositions are attached to products and services. But when you're a salesperson, you also have to sell yourself.

TeleTech, a managed service provider, performed some analysis to demonstrate the "you" value case.[1] The company reports that 75 percent of customers base their purchasing decisions on how well you communicate knowledge and value.

1. 21% of buyers list **credibility** as important to convincing them to buy.
2. 20% emphasize **expertise,** or subject knowledge.
3. 19% care that salespeople **listen** to their needs and concerns.
4. 17% say that **communicating value** is essential to securing their support and business.

Further, the value relationship between you and the buyer is becoming increasingly important to surrounding the job. Buyers make a purchase when you **understand them** and their situation (30 percent); **offer the best solution** for a real problem (29 percent); **develop "chemistry"** (25 percent); and **navigate company politics** deftly (16 percent).

TeleTech also exposes the reasons salespeople lost sales. Unsurprisingly, poor communication skills top the list.

1. 25% of buyers hesitate to buy due to **poor listening skills.**
2. 23% dismiss a salesperson because of a **lack of expertise.**
3. 16% cite **poor preparation** as detrimental to the seller-buyer relationship and potential sale.
4. Rounding out the list, buyers grow leery when

[1] Griffith, Peter. "B2B Customers Want Relationships, Not Sales." July 2015. TeleTech Consulting. Access October 2016. <http://www.teletech.com/resources/articles/b2b-customers-want-relationships-not-sales#.WEgn0qIrKre>.

salespeople **talk about themselves** too much (10 percent); are **unresponsive** (10 percent); and **lack awareness** about the business and the buyer's situation (8 percent).

A buyer might think the product's great. They might even seem to be headed toward a sale. But you'll lose them to another salesperson if you don't establish your value, so develop it even as you make the case for your product or service.

Stakeholder Consensus

Communicating value to different stakeholders, as with the subcontractor and owner, is critical to building consensus.

> **Consensus** is general or widespread agreement, usually among dissimilar parties. Winning all the votes.

As applied to decision-making, consensus means that everyone involved in the selection process supports your proposed solution. It isn't about getting a majority. Consensus is a matter of getting all the votes.

Think of consensus as though you're building a team. To create and manage that team, you listen and take into account everyone's ideas, concerns, and goals. Then, and only then, do you issue a sales proposal.

If you've done the work right, the entire team will agree with you They won't bicker, compromise, or ask for another meeting. They've bought into your solution because you understood their context, asking probing questions, and developed an answer that meets their present and future needs.

You must aim for consensus, especially when dealing with large sales. Without consensus, you'll lose the sales order. The team members will scatter to their positions, even the ones who once seemed to be such staunch supporters. You must, MUST, achieve consensus among stakeholders. It's the only way to ensure everyone goes home happy with their Porsches and Cadillacs.

Closing Thoughts

You might not like chess – maybe you are a checkers person – but bear with me...to keep conversation centered on value, you must be ready for what will happen four moved down the road.

You know that an executive will balk at the price. Maybe someone will object to the timeline. If you can identify those issues ahead of time, you will make the right play when it counts. The concerns become inconsequential because the stakeholders are playing your game, and you always win. Checkmate.

We covered four key ideas in this chapter:

1. Long-term Value
2. Short-term Value
3. Your Value
4. Stakeholder Consensus

All four are critical to surrounding the job. By understanding and identifying that some stakeholders stress short- or long-term value, you can deliver information that develops consensus and secures the assumptive close.

Exercise 2: Keep Conversations Centered on Value

"Sales is like chess. You have to think four steps ahead."

The moment a sales conversation drifts from value, you lose. A salesperson slithers in with a lower price point. A competitor promises to provide a product or service fast. If you don't take control of the conversation immediately, you will lower your price, make impossible assurances, or drop out of the conversation altogether.

You can control that conversation and return it to where it should be – centered squarely on value! Let me show you how in five steps.

1. Build Your Value Proposition

When you come to the sales table, you could be the David in the equation. That doesn't matter. Your size and name recognition do not necessarily guarantee the sale.

You value proposition does. While the Goliaths might have an easier time of stating their value, they still have to state it. And that gives you an opportunity. Lob your stone and topple the giant.

To build your value proposition, you should begin with "why".

- Why are you the best choice?
- Why should people trust you?
- Why are you better than the competition?

Maybe you offer the same service or product as the competitors, but some quality differentiates you. Use it to develop a unique value proposition that can be tailored to a variety of conversations, business use cases, and sales orders.

2. Practice Your Pitch

Once you figure out the value proposition, practice it. No one believes that guy who stammers his way through an 11-second introduction or hems and haws about product specifications.

They lock to the person who speaks with confidence. This person knows she's the best, and she conveys the quality in every word and gesture. So, practice. Practice at networking events. Practice with a mentor. Practice with your dog. Just practice!

3. Put Your Value Proposition in the Buyer's Language

With the value proposition set and practiced, focus on adapting it to specific stakeholders. You accomplish the task before and during sales conversations with a couple of questions, some of which bear similarities to the "why" ones, above.

Before the meeting, ask:

- How will the stakeholder use the product or service?
- How does it affect the person I'm currently speaking to? For example, the CIO versus the field technician.
- What factors and values do my stakeholder care about most?
- How is the product or service different from what the stakeholder currently uses?
- What is that difference worth in quantitative and qualitative terms?

With these questions, write down as many answers as possible. Don't think about the answers too much – get them onto the paper or screen first.

Once you have a list of answers, examine them. Some will be nonsense, but others will give you a strong advantage during face-to-face meetings. They offer talking points, ranging from reduced costs and streamlined operations to increased productivity and profit margins.

Mark Hunter, author of "High-Profit Selling: Win the Sale without Compromising on Price," puts the sales situation this way. "Customers [stakeholders] don't buy anything. They only invest. If we believe this – and I do – then every purchase must result in a return on investment. Customers may argue this is why they need a lower price, but when they do this, they are overlooking the **real value** (emphasis added) of outcomes."[2]

During the meeting, ask:

---

[2] Hunter, Mark. "6 Critical Ways to Show Value Your Customers." Salesforce Blog. Sept. 2013. Accessed December 2016. <https://www.salesforce.com/blog/2013/09/customer-value.html>.

- How would my solution change things for your business or organization?
- How would my solution set you apart from the competition?

Even if you don't use those exact questions, you should focus on asking open-ended ones. You don't want to "lead the witness". You want unbiased answers so that you can better guide the conversation and communicate value.

4. Provide Evidence
Now that you have your talk down, work on the evidence. Maybe you do have the best product in the marketplace, but you have to back the claim. Anything less is "clickbait," and it will get you banished from the sales table.

You should always enter the room with evidence and examples to share. They build credibility and support your value proposition. They can also sway people toward your viewpoint.

Plus, some stakeholders will never be wooed with words. They require hard numbers. Others resonate with testimonials, benchmarks, videos, and documented best practices. You should use all your available resources in order to secure value and surround the job.

5. Share Your Value Proposition All the Time
I once heard an ad agency executive say, "You'll get tired of the creative long before the public does." The statement is true in the advertising word, and it holds true in ours. We'll tire of spouting our value proposition long before the stakeholder wearies of hearing it.

State and restate your value proposition everywhere. Also, remember that even though you're saying the same thing over and over again, that doesn't mean you have to use the exact-same words or examples. Shake things up. Use whatever words and evidence is necessary to draw the stakeholder toward the sale.

Examples of Value by Role

Owner
In construction, owners never build ugly or cheap buildings. So if you believe that, buying products with good quality at the right price is what's important. Establishing a good quality reputation is important.

IT Department
Whatever it may be, in a building or a company that they own, whether the IT department is the buyer or it is bought by someone else, everyone will look to them to maintain it and answer questions about it. What is important to them is (a) compatibility and (b) control. They want to make sure that whatever is going to be purchased works with their current IT ecosystem and they either have the skills or can find the skills easily to maintain it.

Sales Manager
Sales Managers get judged on numbers, so how can whatever you are selling them help them get to their goals, so they can get that bonus.

CHAPTER THREE
Define your Influencers

"You don't understand."

Anytime I hear the words, "You don't understand," I know I'm on the right track. I encounter this phrase all the time, and it rarely means that I don't understand. I do understand, but my message isn't hitting home. I have to rethink my approach so that the stakeholder can hear what I have to say.

Don't be afraid of the words, "You don't understand." The three words typically mean you're getting through to your stakeholder. You just face some signal interference. To get past it, you'll need to either press for a more in-depth answer or help the people at the table discover and share one.

View Stakeholders as Influencers
The key to breaking through the noise comes from understanding that stakeholders are more than stock characters in a company. They are influencers. They affect not only purchasing decisions and company

direction, but also their peers and employers.

Influencers are individuals who impact other people's purchasing decisions because of their authority, knowledge, position, or relationships. In the B2B world, this role can be filled by internal employees and external consultants.

In some ways, influencers are like a stack of dominoes. If you "influence" one to your way of thinking, they could topple nearby game pieces. Accomplishing that requires you to learn what influences them or, to put it another way, what causes them to think and act the way they do. If you can do that, you will be able to successfully surround them and leverage their power.

Look for Common Traits among the Influencers

But, what factors influence people? People want to make a profit. They hope to be liked. They want to achieve Steve Job's-like prestige. They wish to be remembered long after the grave is dug, and the hole is filled.

Influencers are like history – they repeat themselves. So, if you want to know what affects a stakeholder or company, start with the past. Research where the company works, what it has purchased, and why.

Also know that most influential elements fall into distinct and relatively broad categories. If you can identify the influence and map it to a category, you will be better prepared for conversations. You will also hold a stronger position with your stakeholders. They beleive that you understand their unique needs, wants, and pressures, so they listen to you and come to you when they need assistance or advice.

Five Common Influences

I've run across the following five influences more times than I can count: **money, vision, investment, legacy,** and **ego**. Most people are an amalgamation of influences, not one alone. However, one factor trends to dominate their thoughts and actions.

If you can isolate the "one", you can use it to convince stakeholders to buy your product or service. You're now explaining the purchase in reasons and motivations intuitive to them. Of course, they're going to buy from you. Your solution makes the most sense.

1. **Money.** Money means paycheck. It influences people in all sorts of ways, sometimes for the good and sometimes for the bad. Most of the time, it produces a scarcity mindset with stakeholders focusing on pinching pennies or worrying about how to meet payroll after investing in a new technology or service.

2. **Vision.** A stakeholder's vision influences how they see the world and your proffered solution. If it doesn't mesh with their vision, they will bid you good luck and farewell. The scope of the vision and its subsequent influence typically varies by person and position.

3. **Investment.** A person influenced by investment may seem similar to the money people, but they differ greatly. The investment influencer looks to the future, while the money one fixates on the present. The two influences

converge at times. For example, both the
money and the investment influencer likely will
want to see financial projections.

4. **Legacy.** The legacy influence sometimes
    offers the greatest opportunity to communicate
    value. The stakeholder heavily influenced by it
    desires to leave the world a better place or to
    create a company that outlasts them. As
    investment and money coincide at times, so do
    legacy and vision.

5. **Ego.** Ego sometimes connotes pride, but as an
    influence, it relates to the person's makeup.
    Their history, biases, personalities, and need
    for recognition, control, or comfort affect how
    they perceive you and your product.
    Deciphering this influence can be challenging,
    but it offers great rewards. If you tap into a
    person's ego, you have discovered what
    makes them tick at a deep, deep level. At that
    point, it becomes relatively easy to sway them
    to your way of thinking.

Appeal to the Influences to Surround the Job

To surround the sale, you must know what affects your
stakeholders. The stakeholders can be grouped into four
categories.

Top Level

Top-level stakeholders tend to be owners, presidents,
founders, and chief executive officers (CEOs). They
care about dollar signs and profits, buy you generally
find a stronger desire to cast a vision or leave a
legacy.

Ego can also play a large role, if not the largest one. Most entrepreneurs don't start a business without high levels of confidence and grit. Discover which influence holds the majority and cater to it to win the sale.

Senior Level
Senior-level stakeholders serve as chief financial officers (CFOs), chief information officers (CIOs), chief safety (and compliance) officers (CSOs), and other executives who report to the CEO or president. Other senior level stakeholders, depending on the project, include architects, designers, and engineers.

Influences vary widely among this group. The CFO and CIO care about protecting the company's pocketbook and public image. Ego may be present, too, especially when dealing with designers and architects. They sometimes display a more "artistic" sensibility or a desire to be known for their work. Even engineers can demonstrate an egotistical streak when they get into technical specifications and mathematical equations.

Mid Level
Mid-level influences are managers and contractors. While the top- and senior-level stakeholders may make the final decisions, the managers and contractors enact it.

This group of people often cares about delivering projects on time and under budget. They may also be more focused on the day-to-day workflows or feel pressured to improve operational efficiency and financial reports.

Ground Floor
The ground floor refers to people who install products and services. It can also include the people who use the items on a daily basis, as well as sales representatives.

Like the other groups, you may see a variety of influences with ground-floor employees. Money often is one, but don't neglect the others. Many employees hope to move into mid- and upper-management roles. Others care about doing good work so as to set an example or to receive approval from their peers or upper management.

By encountering stakeholders through their influences, you shift the conversation away from price (or some other factor) to a quality that truly matters to them. That quality, though, is up to you to discover. It could be legacy, ego, or money. Whatever the quality is, use it to surround the sale and gain the assumptive close.

Turn Influencers into Allies
If figuring out what influences people sounds like a lot of work, it is. Discovering and deciphering influential factors takes time, effort, and diligence. However, the work's critical to surrounding the job.

When you converse with influencers through their priorities, they become allies, people committed to your product or service. They do the hard work of selling for you, convincing other influencers to buy your solution.

The television show "Bull" encapsulates the idea well.[3]

---

[3] Bull. 2016-present. CBS. Accessed November 2016. <http://www.imdb.com/title/tt5827228/>.

Bull and his team perform "trial science" to understand jurors and their perspective on the defendant. The team spends the show shifting that perspective by catering to people's influences.

For some jurors, their peers' opinions matter most. Others display well-developed egos. They have to be pulled toward Bull's outlook in order to affect the rest of the jury pool. Some jurors are convinced by statistics. Some just want to be liked and accepted.

Whatever the influence, Bull's team finds it and capitalizes on it. They change the jury's mind by focusing on what drives the individual. As a result, Bull and their defendant get the desired verdict.

You can do the same with your stakeholders. Seek to understand what motivates them, what "influences" them. Once you have that information, use it. It'll win them to you and your product or service.

Remember You're an Influence

But, take caution. You will lose people if you forget **you are an influencer.** You, because of perceived or real authority, knowledge, experience, position, or relationship, hold influence.

This means you can guide stakeholders toward or away from your product or service. Think of the situation as being like a chemistry experiment. If you measure the elements correctly, the experiment works as expected. If you don't or aren't paying quite enough attention, the experiment backfires.

You are a catalyst in the sales process. Your presence

positively or negatively charges stakeholders, either attracting or alienating them. Because of that, you should seek to understand what influences you. Then and only then will you see the element – YOU – to achieve desired results time and time again.

Closing Thoughts

We spanned a couple of ideas in this chapter, beginning with a general discussion about influencers. An influencer is anyone, internal or external to the company, who can impact the final outcome. They may hold power over the decision and other people because of power, personality, perspective, or responsibility.

Influencers, though, do not exist in a vacuum. They influence, yes, but they also are influenced upon. Some influencers may want to be liked. Others wish to be known for their leadership and innovation. Many influences exist, but five are most common.

1. Money
2. Vision
3. Investment
4. Legacy
5. Ego

We then discussed four groups of people you'll interact with then surrounding the job.

1. Top-level
2. Senior-level
3. Mid-Level
4. Ground Floor

The people in those groups hold votes in the final

purchasing decision. Because of that, you should work inside all four groups. Identify the influencers in each and get their votes so that they achieve consensus concerning the buying decision.

We concluded this chapter with some thoughts on allies and personal influence. You want allies. Allies are stakeholders who believe in your product and service. As a result, they make your case for you, often reaching the stakeholders who never seem to have the time for a meeting or a 15-minute informational call. They can also speed up the sales process, delivering the assumptive close faster than expected.

You also want to remember your influence. You have some, be it for good or ill. You should seek self-awareness about not only how much you impact others but also what influences you. If you do, you will conduct more productive conversations that lead to more surrounded jobs.

Exercise 3: Map the Stakeholders and Influences

"Sales is not a hobby."

For this exercise, I'm going to ask you to write some things down. Words on a page simplify matters and help build practical and achievable plans. There are 2 ways of doing this: (a) graphically, on a spreadsheet or (b) visually, with circle diagrams.

a) Graphically

Graphical representation is the easier of the 2 methods. It allows you to track each sales position in a spreadsheet, so you can have a holistic and simplistic view of what influences each stakeholder. But it has limitations. You do not know to what degree each stakeholder is influenced by each category. In the next exercise, you will see how I use a circle to represent these degrees of influence.

Using a basic spreadsheet, list influencers and mark off columns of what influences them. This is dynamic and changes as you get to know the influencers. Some preconceived influences will be confirmed while others will change.

	Owner	Enterprise Architect	Consultant	Line of Business User	Business Analyst
Money	X				
Vision		X	X	X	X
Investment	X				
Legacy		X			
Ego		X			

Figure 2. Graphically Matching Stakeholders with their Influences Example

b) Visually

As mentioned above, we will be drawing circles. These circles will allow you to see to what degree who is influenced by what.

First, write down the **categories** of the people in your sales pipeline. The categories should include at least these four: **Top-level**, **Senior-level**, **Mid-level**, and the **Ground Floor**.

Second, write down the **stakeholders** found within those categories. The CEO and CFO are obvious choices but don't neglect the executive assistants. They guard the CEO and other executives from salespeople. To reach those executives, you have to make it past their gatekeepers first.

Third, add people's names beside the positions. Names remind you that stakeholders are people. Plus, the names will help later on in this exercise.

Finished with the list? Good. Set it aside for a moment so that I can ask you a question: How many degrees are in a circle? This question usually earns me blank stares during trainings and presentations, so I'll share the right answer with you: 360 degrees! Now, you can parse those degrees any way you like, but they always add up to 360.

We're going to use that principle with the circle, giving some influencer categories and stakeholder positions more degrees than others. The executive assistant, after all, has some impact on whether you get through the door, but they probably have little say when it comes to purchasing decisions. You can account or that difference by using three circles, as I did in chapter two.

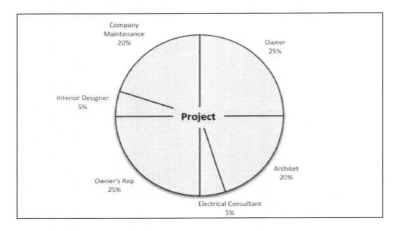

Figure 3. Visually Matching Stakeholders with their Influences Example

With your circle segmented, you quickly see who holds the most influence in the room and over the purchasing decision. You should use that information in a couple of ways.

1. Get to Know your Influencers
First, you should use the circle to research our influencers. Start with the larger influencers and work your way around the first circle. Figure out what matters to each influencer and how they establish value. Store that information somewhere, whether on a circle itself or in your notes. It

will come in handy for telephone calls, emails, and in-person meetings, as well as revising your second and third iterations of the circles as you glean more information and understanding.

2. Tailor our Value Proposition
Second, you should use the circles to determine your approach to influencers and sales meetings, that is, you should let them direct your value proposition and talking points. The circles tell you where to focus attention and how to speak and act to surround the jobs.

Closing Thoughts
I like the circle exercise because it gets us away from gut reactions and instinct. Some salespeople might be able to rely on those things, but I don't recommend it. Sales is a process, not a hobby, and that means there's an art and a science to it. The drawing of a circle proves the point. It gives an objective view of the potential sale, clarifies your position, and identifies what you need to do next to surround the job and get the assumptive close.

CHAPTER FOUR

Control the Outcome with Knowledge

"He that holds the knowledge controls the decision."

Consumers, on both the B2B and B2C sides, are more informed than ever before. They consult large number of sources, with popular ones including supplier websites, Google, product and service review sites, corporate blogs, social media, and third-party websites, long before speaking with you.

Avanade's study, "Global Survey: B2B is the New B2C," finds the following about B2B customers and their purchasing decisions.[4]

- An increasing number of enterprise buyers display consumer-like behaviors, with **61 percent** stating that third-party sites and recommendations from business peers and partners, industry influencers,

---

[4] Avanade. "Global Survey: B2B is the New B2C, The Consumerization of Enterprise Sales." November 2013. Avanade. Accessed December 2016. <https://www.avanade.com/~/media/asset/research/the-new-customer-journey-global-study.pdf>

and social networks impact their final purchasing decision.

- B2B buyers also report that the customer experience, not the price, affects their choice of vendor. **56 percent** of surveyed respondents say that a positive experience, which includes the vendor's knowledge of their business and its needs, not only influences their decision to buy also makes them more willing to pay a higher price for products and services.

Accenture's study, "2014 State of B2B Procurement Study: Uncovering the Shifting Landscape in B2B Commerce,"[5] echoes Avanade's. The company's survey of B2B buyers with annual purchasing budgets of more than $100,000 reports similar sentiments.

- **44 percent** of respondents say they research companies and products on connected devices like laptops, tablets, and smartphones.
- **94 percent** conduct online research before making a corporate purchase.
- The online research occurs regardless of price point. **40 percent** of B2B buyers research goods costing below $10,000. **31 percent** assess goods costing equal to or greater than $10,000.

But as a salesperson, you must be able to meet

---

[5] Accenture. "2014 State of B2B Procurement Study: Uncovering the Shifting Landscape in BB Commerce." 2014. Accenture. Accessed December 2016. <https://www.accenture.com/t20150624T211502_w_/us-en/Accenture/Converstion-Asset/DotCom/Documents/Global/PDF/Industries_15/Accenture-B2B Procurement Study.pdf>

stakeholders wherever they are in their purchasing journeys. You don't have the luxury of waiting around for stakeholders to come to you. You have to go to them, no matter how informed or uninformed they are. According to McKinsey, "It's not enough to identify the decision maker in an organization. For [...] sales activities to be effective, companies need to focus on those points in the decision journey where they can be most successful in influencing those decision makers."[6]

That need requires you to become the most knowledgeable person in the room. By arming yourself with knowledge, you turn into the most valuable person at the sales meeting. You, not the stakeholder, are a rich repository of information and relevant, actionable advice and insights.

In addition to enhancing your value, knowledge grows your influence. Stakeholders grow aware of your expertise and ability to develop customized solutions that solve real business problems. As a result, they come to you more and more often for information and assistance.

In McKinsey's research, "Do You Really Understand How Your Business Customers Buy?",[7] getting to know your stakeholders' purchasing behaviors, needs, and cycles leads to the following positive results.

---

[6] McKinsey. "The B2B Customer Decision Journey: The Route to Increased Sales." April 2013. McKinsey. Accessed November 2016. <http://www.forbes.com/sites/mckinsey/2013/04/24/the-b2b-customer-decision-journey-the-route-to-increased-sales/#6be64b1d275a>
[7] McKinsey. "Do You Really Understand How Your Business Customers Buy?" February 2015. McKinsey Quarterly. Accessed December 2016. <http://www.mckinsey.com/business-functions/marketing-and-sales/our-insights/do-you-really-understand-how-your-business-customers-buy>

- New customer leads increase by **20 percent**
- First-time customers grow by **10 percent**
- The time between qualifying leads and closing deals can speed up by as much as **20 percent**

Knowledge, simply put, performs a supporting and critical function in surrounding the sale. It enriches the sales process, bolsters your ability to identify influencers, and establishes your value.

To achieve that type of influence, you will need to recognize that knowledge is two-fold. It's (1) all the things you know and (2) all the things you communicate.

First things first, whenever you meet with a stakeholder, they need to know what other influencers you have spoken to. Communicating this fact accomplishes three things:

1. You demonstrate you have worked the project to the fullest.
2. You understand everyone's role in the project.
3. You offer greater insight and value because you've met with all the influencers.

If you emphasize anything in this chapter, emphasize the second point, communication. It helps you influence the influencers. It also makes you one of the team because you are connected to and knowledgeable about all the influencers.

Finally, it helps with achieving consensus among the influencers. Many of them will initially tell you they don't make the buying decision. Others may consult with the primary decision maker before solidifying their opinion.

Others may consult with the primary decision maker before solidifying their own opinion. Don't get caught up in the intricacies of that. Your goal is to position yourself – via knowledge – with all the influencers so that when they are asked for their votes, they unanimously vote for you and your product or service.

Become Your Customers' Knowledge Center

A knowledge center performs as a central hub of information, ideas, and resources When you turn yourself into one, you become essential to the customer and their purchasing decision. You contain everything they need, from the answer to a seemingly random, pulled-from-the-ether question to queries about ROI and profit projections.

You should also remember that you still play a critical role in the sales cycle. B2B customers may spend more time researching products and services. They most likely will continue to do so, throughout the sales process. However, your knowledge moves them toward you and away from your competitors.

Customers can compare prices, product features, and reviews all day long. They sometimes struggle to make sense of the information. And that's where you come in.

Customers need you to guide them through the sales process, which can be convoluted and complex. You also claim an external perspective on the company. Use it. Your outside knowledge, awareness, and insights can produce unique business cases that deliver results and build toward future efforts.

Salesforce discuss the role of increased information and knowledge centers in their article, "Selling to the Modern

B2B Buyer."[8] The organization offers this advice:

B2B buyers look for vendors who understand their pain points and are knowledgeable about the industry. Sales reps should be **subject matter experts** in their field and should be able to convey the information to prospects in a clear and concise manner. They should also be able to provide perspective on the market and help the prospects interpret and apply this information to their own situation and challenges.

SiriusDecisions, Inc., a global B2B research and advisory firm, strengthens Salesforce's argument. SiriusDecisions's research into B2B buying behaviors and processes shows that salespeople are **not** "being displaced by the ubiquity of digital."[9] Rather, B2B buyers continue to rely on one-on-one vendor relationships.

Jennifer Ross, Senior Research Director of CMO Strategies at SiriusDecisions, says business purchasers employ more "human-to-human interactions [...] at higher expenditure levels, but even in lower-priced offerings [...] personal interactions occur."

The latest research from Demand Gen, "The 2016 B2B Buyer's Survey Report," concludes the matter.[10] The

---

[8] Salesforce. "Selling to the Modern B2B Buyer." Une 2016. Salesforce. Accessed November 2016. <https://www.salesforce.com/blog/2016/06/selling-to-the-modern-b2b-buyer.html>

[9] SiriusDecisions, Inc. "SiriusDecisions Summit 2015: B2B Buying Methodology Debunked." May 2015. Demand Gen. Accessed December 2016. <http://www.demandgenreport.com/features/industry-insights/siriusdecisions-summit-2015-b2b-buying-mythlogy-debunked>

[10] Demand Gen. "2016 B2B Buyer's Survey Report." June 2016. Demand Gen. Accessed December 2016.

report finds, "Buyers overwhelmingly gravitate toward companies that demonstrate 'a **stronger knowledge** of the company and its needs.'"

- **97 percent** of surveyed B2B buyers choose a vendor who demonstrates a stronger knowledge of the solution area and the business landscape.
- **94 percent** choose a vendor who shows a stronger knowledge of the purchaser's company and its needs.
- **90 percent** select vendors because they provide content that proves ROI or build a use case for the product or service in question.

Your role as a knowledgeable person is critical, to both the company where you work and the stakeholders and influencers you serve. To turn yourself into that knowledgeable salesperson, follow these four steps:

1. Make Yourself Essential
When a daughter's washing machine breaks, she rarely calls the repair guy. She calls the person most critical to her and the immediate problem – usually her mom or dad. She needs someone to tell her what to do, now.

You play that "parent" role in the sales process. You hold information critical to making an informed decision, and the stakeholder knows it. In addition, you're knowledgeable. Use your knowledge to help stakeholders and influencers traverse the purchasing decision. You also possess expertise about the larger market. You should employ it to develop insightful

---

<ttp://www.demandgenreport.com/resources/research/2016-b2b-buyer-s-survey-report>

solutions, forecast potential impacts, and continue establishing value so that you are what every other solution is compared to.

Also consider that you, like a parent, might not have all the facts when an influencer calls in hysterics. You, however, can calm and win them by talking a little, listening a lot, and asking the right questions. Doing so will make you indispensable to the customer. When they need something, anything, they come to you and you alone for the information.

2. Talk, but Not Too Much
In Chapter two, we looked at some reasons salespeople lose the sale. One of them is talking too much. Salespeople often speak about themselves or the product or service to the detriment of the sale and their reputation. Salespeople may be egomaniacs – we kind of have to be to do what we do – but we need to curb the ego slightly when attempting to turn ourselves into knowledge centers.

If it helps, think back to when you pursued a romance with someone special. You probably didn't score points on the dates where you talked about you, yourself, and you. The ones that led to lengthier, more enjoyable relationships arose from talking less and listening more.

Stakeholders and influencers are not different. They remember salespeople who know when to talk and when to listen. For them, it is the better part of service. For you, it's integral to developing an in-depth knowledge about the stakeholder, the company and its needs. So, talk, but not too much.

3. Listen, then Listen Some More

Listening doesn't happen if you're always talking. Obvious point, but it needs to be made. I've seen many salespeople talk themselves out of orders simply because they didn't know when to shut up.

A better approach is found in listening. It shows a wise restraint. It's also sensible and logical. If you want to be the most knowledgeable person in the room, you've got to listen at some point, and learn.

Nobody learns anything when one person, you or someone else, monopolizes the conversation. Talk, yes, but also listen. Let people respond to your questions to see if you truly understand the problem or need. It's amazing what they'll share if you'll just listen and let them talk.

4. Keep Asking Questions

In chapter three, I said I sometimes have to dig for better answers or help customers discover the answers for themselves. Informed questions are how I accomplish the task. By listening well, I ask better questions and subsequently receive better replies.

Questions result from the push-and-pull of talking and listening. The work creates a tension necessary to get to the right questions and right answers. You prod, encourage, and nod when needed – whatever it takes to keep asking questions and receiving answers in return.

The process turns me – and you – into problem-solvers, and stakeholders, no matter their position in the organization, love problem-solvers. Problem-solvers make their jobs easier and help them see a future in which your product or service plays a part.

Examples from the Road

I was sitting in an owner's office with the local salesperson and we were looking to close an order for a large building control system. We reviewed our points, and all together agreed that we should get a Purchase Order from another person in the office. This was good, we got the commitment and we all agreed on the major points. Job done...you would think.

At this moment, as I went to stand up with the intention of shaking hands with the owner and thanking her. In the moment of silence while getting up, the local salesperson says, "Wait till I show you the new proposed technology we are coming out with!" I almost threw up. Why say that? Why open a new door that doesn't exist? Why? Why? Why?

The owner says, "Well let's hold off until you can show me this, you know I wouldn't want old technology in my building." Of course, she doesn't! No one does. The only problem is we didn't have any new technology coming, it was just a conversation with a design engineer over lunch when they said they were looking at potential new products down the road.

The salesperson talked their way out of an order or at least postponed the order AND stated a conversation he couldn't finish.

"Once you have the order, SHUT UP and LEAVE!"

Closing Thoughts

We covered a lot of information in this chapter about how knowledge helps your surround the job. B2B buyers may be more informed than ever before, but they still turn to you for knowledge and expertise.

Knowledge is your ally. The information and influencers you know secures your seat at the sales table. Never lose sight of that fact. You help stakeholders grow their businesses and alleviate day-to-day inefficiencies. You solve problems that they can't unscramble without you.

Now, get out there. Identify your influencers, establish your value, make yourself a knowledge center, and listen. Do those four things and you will gain the assumptive close.

CHAPTER FIVE

Win the Sale by Getting All the Votes

"You can never have too many votes."

In 1972, Richard Nixon ascended to the White House with a landslide victory – almost earning 25 percent of the electoral vote.[11] His economic policy and finesse with foreign affairs made him a popular candidate with the Electoral College.

George McGovern, this Democratic opponent, couldn't hope to capture those votes. He championed an anti-war rhetoric that appealed to the American people, but his outsider status and scandalous running mate, Thomas Eagleton, stood as stumbling blocks within the Electoral College. As a result, he lost to the competition.

Other elections, including Eisenhower's 1952 victory and Lyndon B. Johnson's slam-dunk in 1964, follow similar

---

[11] For more information about how the Electoral College influences elections, visit the Pew Research Center.
<http://www.pewresearch.org/fact-tank/2016/12/20/why-electoral-college-landslides-are-easier-to-win-than-popular-vote-ones/>

landslide patterns. The expected and sometimes unexpected candidates enter the White House. They did so for a singular reason: they captured more votes in the right places.

They might not have secured all the votes, but they tried. They knew that the more votes you have, the more likely it is that you'll win. The same principle applies to you. When you have all the votes needed to surround a sale, the sale becomes a matter of when rather than if.

Establish Who Your Voters Are

I sometimes use "voters" in lieu of words like "stakeholders" and "influencers". It keeps people from getting caught up in "stakeholders" versus "influencers" and losing focus on surrounding the job.

Don't mistake me here – identifying stakeholders and influencers is important. But using the term "voters" helps me move back toward the bigger picture, the sale and the assumptive close.

A **landslide victory** is when one candidate or party takes the majority of the votes in the elected body, all but decimating the opposition. The subsequent victory seems settled before the dust settles, clearly achieving the assumptive close.

The term "votes" and "voters" also reminds me that every influencer has a vote to cast. My job, and yours, is to secure those votes. We do that by establishing value, identifying pitfalls, seeking out influencers, examining the surrounding influences, and growing our knowledge.

"Votes" also recalls that some votes possess more weight

than others. The electoral season demonstrates that point. A candidate might seem like a shoe-in in terms of the popular vote, but they must gain a greater number of electoral votes. They subsequently win the political race and begin their term in office.

If you ever start to forget the role of votes in closing a sale, think of the U.S. president. Stakeholders and influencers hold votes integral to surrounding and closing the sale. As such, they possess the power to bring you into or keep you out of "office".

Define Voters' Relationships to the Sale

But getting all the votes isn't always easy. The smallest cry of concern from one voter can cause the others to waiver. It happens all the time during electoral cycles. The campaign seems to be moving along smoothly until one accusation or concern jerks it to a halt.

The same can occur at the sales table. An accusation might not be lobbed, but a concern could be raised. If you aren't prepared for it, your work to surround the job could fall apart. And the competition won't stand idly by. They'll swoop in and take advantage of your vulnerability.

To prevent the scenario, you must enter the room prepared. Learn to expect the concerns. Anticipate them by getting to know your influencers and understanding their level of voting power. You can circumvent many problems simply by raising and solving issues before a voter gives voice to them.

If you've been following the process outlined in this book, you've already completed much of that work. You identified influencers and the factors that influence the.

You know a lot about these people, what makes them tick and how much of a vote they have. Some may have a lot of voting power. They're more like an Electoral College vote. Others have less and perform similarly to popular votes.

> N.B. If you haven't already, complete **Exercise 3: Map the Stakeholders and Influences.** The circle acts as a map when it comes to influencers and votes. Every influencer takes a piece of the "pie". Your job is to understand how much of it they take and to use that information to successfully surround the job.

Don't dismiss those "popular" votes, though. They could influence the outcome. When it comes to votes, you want all of them. The more votes you have, the more sales you will close. You can never have too many votes.

Capture All the Votes

Capturing all the votes encompasses activities discussed previously. You will need to establish value, that of yourself and the product or service you represent. You will also need to understand how people see and relate to value.

Thinking of the process as a campaign can be helpful. If you know how people perceive value, you can address them on a personal level. You accomplish that work by reviewing a company's history and meeting with stakeholders. Through those conversations, you learn about the organization and its concerns about their industry and financial future. As a result, you become better able to speak their language and to communicate value via targeted solutions and insights.

The work doesn't end there. Once you establish value,

you will need to seek out stakeholders and influencers. Request to have meetings with them. Ask questions and listen to their answers. The name of the game is knowledge now, and if you want to surround the sale, you must become the most knowledgeable person in the room.

Knowledge, not personality, confirms your position with voters and makes you invulnerable to attack from competitors. You can be the most charismatic salesperson out there, but if you don't know what you're talking about or what your voters need, you'll lose the sale. Knowledge is power. It gets the landslide victory.

Examples from the Road
When talking to the owner of a building, he tells us that the architect's brother-in-law is a purchasing manager. He gives us the purchasing managers' name and number but doesn't want us to reference that we know who his brother-in-law is.

We call the purchasing manager and tell him the owner gave us his name and want to meet with him to review what we showed the owner and that the architected specified us.

So what does all of this tell me?

1. The architect has a brother-in-law that will do the purchasing
2. The owner confides in us the relationship
3. We make sure the purchasing manager knows we have a relationship with the owner AND the architect.

We contact the architect to let him know we met with the owner and tell him any comments he made about our products. We also mention that we are meeting the purchasing manager and ask who else we should meet with.

In the end, all of this helped us secure all the votes and win the assumptive close.

Closing Thoughts

In this chapter, we looked at what voters are, what they aren't and why they're important. We also discussed how you obtain their votes – generally through the steps detailed in earlier chapters. You win votes by establishing value, identifying influencers, and becoming a knowledge center.

But if you take only one lesson away from this chapter, take this one: **stakeholders and influencers are voters.** Some votes count for a lot, and some count for a little. They all count for something. Because of that, you should aim to get all the votes. You can never have too many votes.

Exercise Four: Establish Trust and Authority with Knowledge

"Money talks and bullshit walks."

If you want to close sales, you have to say the right words and back those words with expertise, insight, and evidence. People trust people who know what they're talking about. They buy from them, be it a small purchase such as a pair of loafers or a complex one, like lighting equipment or business software.

To help establish your trust and authority, I've provided a list of items to know below. It is NOT a checklist, though you may use it that way. The list is meant to get you thinking about what you know and don't know. As such, it should either identify gaps in your knowledge or jumpstart a customized list that works for you and your product or service.

1. Outcomes
  - What does the customer hope will happen if they work with you?
  - What quantifiable and quantitative results do they demand?

2. Budget
- What's the perceived value of the project?
- How is it broken down by costs for products, labor, implementation, etc.?
- What happens if the project goes over budget?

3. Product Budget
- How much is your product budget?
- Can you provide samples?
- If not, what other information and resources can you leave behind to build a business use case for your solution?

4. Budget Ownership
- Who establishes the budget?
- What are their roles?
- How much influence do they have?
- What's their voting power?
- Do they own the project or only the budget?

5. Timeline
- What is the stakeholder's timeline?
- How does it tie to their expectations and sense of value?
- What happens if the project goes over time?

6. Size
- How big is the project?
- How many buildings will it cover?
- How many people will it impact?
- Which people?
- Will the project require closing off sections of building?
- If so, how long?
- Where will the people who work in that cordoned-off section go during the implementation phase?

7. People
- Who will manage the project day-to-day?
- What promises on delivery can they be held

accountable to?

8. Implementation

- How long will it take for a full rollout to occur?
- How will downtime effect the customer's business or organization?
- What best practices and resources are available to ease the implementation and rollout phases?

9. Forecasting

- What business trends are on the horizon?
- How does your solution mitigate risks found with those trends or take advantage of them?
- What promises can you make about present and future cost-savings or profits?

10. Risk

- How does your company handle risk?
- How does your solution lower the customer's risk?

Closing Thoughts

Conversations with your stakeholders may not cover all 10 areas. They could cover less or more. Regardless, if you spend time asking the right questions, you'll get to the right answers. And those answers are critical. They help you share knowledge, build trust and authority, and surround the job.

CHAPTER SIX
Migrate Risk to Get the Sale

"The devil is in the details."
People mitigate risk every day. They wear seat belts, buckle kids into safety seats, wrap an ankle before working out, and ask a doctor about potential side effects. While those people might not say they're mitigating, that's exactly what they're doing. They're taking steps to manage potential scenarios: a car accident, a torn ligament, or an adverse drug reaction.

Your stakeholders follow the same pattern, albeit on a much larger and more impactful scale. Their purchasing decisions affect hundreds, if not thousands, of people rather than a single person or household. What they decide prevents or spells financial disaster or reputational damage for the company.

Risk Mitigation is the steps taken to reduce the likelihood of adverse effects. Most companies adhere to one or more of four risk management strategies: (1) risk acceptance, (2) risk transference, (3) risk limitation, and (4) risk avoidance.

And that means you must understand how your stakeholders perceive and approach risk. You don't have to be the resident expert when it comes to the particulars of those risks, but you do need to identify them and know who will handle them. Your knowledge of a company's risk can affect whether a stakeholder chooses to work with you or someone else.

Risk Affects Stakeholders and Sales

Risk often becomes the proverbial straw that breaks the camel's back. You may be the most knowledgeable person in the room and you could have established value with the different stakeholders.

But if your knowledge and relationship fail to translate into risk mitigation, you could still lose the sale. Stakeholders, particularly those in upper management, want to know that their investment is a semi-sold bet. They don't and won't fling money about. (At least not usually. They sometimes go on spending sprees as the end of the fiscal year approaches.)

To get inside your stakeholder's mindset, you should review a traditional risk management plan. It comprises of five parts:

1. Risks and consequences outline the perceived risk and its likely repercussions. The risk could relate to time, budget, resources, compliance, or some other issue.
2. Probability often is written as a number on a scale or a percentage. It identifies the likelihood of the risk occurring.
3. Impact defines the repercussions, giving a hard number to the potential fallout. Most companies

use some sort of scale to assess impact.

4.   Priority is the result of multiplying probability by impact. The higher the result, the higher the priority.

5.   Response details the strategy used to eliminate or reduce the defined risk and its possible consequences.

You likely won't be involved with developing those numbers or responses, but you should find out the information. If you know the risks and the priority placed upon them, you can better position your product or service. Your solution could very well reduce or eliminate some of the company's risks.

Risks Common to Stakeholders

Each stakeholder and influencer come with a set of unique circumstances, characteristics, and risks. For that reason, you should converse with everyone about his or her concerns. The solution you ultimately suggest hinges upon the information.

However, that doesn't mean every stakeholder is a unicorn. Stakeholders and influencers hold some risks in common. The list that follows isn't definitive, but it will help decipher what kind of risk you're largely dealing with.

1.   **Finances.** Every stakeholder will at least allude to this risk, although some will care about it more than others.

2.   **Unfamiliarity.** When stakeholders are unfamiliar with you and your product or service, they either will be gung-ho or reluctant.

3.   **Reputation.** Voters put themselves on the line

when they recommend your company, product, or service. They wonder if their recommendation could result in a loss of position or influence.

4. **Operations.** With this risk, the stakeholder worries that implementing your solution could disrupt the supply chain or hamper day-to-day workflows.

5. **Resources.** This concern often pairs with the operations one. The stakeholder fears that productivity and efficiency will tank while people get used to your solution.

6. **Time.** Similar to the resources and operations risks, this concern asks how much time will be spent learning the product or service. Related questions involve time spent researching your solution, as well as implementing it.

7. **Performance.** This risk comes up most often with hardware and software deployments. The stakeholder expresses concern about maintenance, recalls, and retirements.

8. **Physical.** Some businesses and organizations follow stringent safety and compliance standards. The stakeholder fears that your product or service could create a hazardous work environment or result in litigation.

9. **Environmental.** Some stakeholders, particularly international ones, will ask about geopolitical situations, epidemics, and natural disasters. They worry that your solution could falter because of an earthquake or shift in political power.

10. **Execution.** Many stakeholders mention this risk. They question if you can truly implement the solution on time and within budget.

None of these risks are difficult, but you won't discover them without in-depth conversation. Just because you know stakeholders share some risks, generally doesn't mean you know them specifically. You will need to dig for answers until you reach the risks that matter Only then can you offer the correct solution.

Strategies to Mitigate Risk

As stated earlier, businesses typically follow one of four risk mitigation strategies:

1. **Risk Acceptance.** This strategy doesn't reduce risk, but many companies use it. They establish their tolerable level of risk, then invest in projects, products, and services that live within it. They may also use the strategy in two other situations: (1) when approached with a solution whose outcomes outweigh the risks, or (2) when other risk management strategies prove cost-prohibitive.

2. **Risk Avoidance.** With this strategy, organizations avoid risk altogether. The strategy acts as the counterpoint to acceptance. It can often be expensive to practice, perhaps explaining why few businesses invest heavily in it.

3. **Risk Limitation.** Imitation tends to be the most common risk mitigation plan. It seeks to "limit" risk through certain steps and actions, such as contingency plans, enabling agreements, and backup data servers. Usually, the limitation strategy operates as a hybrid of avoidance and acceptance.

4. **Risk Transference.** This strategy sometimes goes by other names, such as shared risk or risk partnership. The customer transfers risk to a

willing third-party, generally one who handles an operational aspect like customer service, payroll, R&D development, or human services. Many businesses use the strategy if the outsourced service isn't one of their core competencies.

If your stakeholder doesn't follow the avoidance strategy, there's hope for the sale yet. You just have to figure out the stakeholder's key objections and offer solutions that resolve them.

For example, stakeholders who pose the "unfamiliar" argument require information. They need to see how the product or service works and be able to envision using it in daily practice. They would also like to hear unbiased reviews from customers.

Stakeholders who raise the money argument simply need financial statements; they only care about the quantitative proof and you have lost the sale. It's about X's and O's, it is not about quality, reputation and the other pieces that make the sale. They want quantitative proof that your product or service will do what you promise it will do. They will be happy if you show metrics and financial forecasts.

Other tactics to mitigate concerns include scope letters and enabling agreements. The first document states what you will supply, i.e., your responsibilities. It also establishes guidelines and boundaries. As such, a scope letter is an opportunity to set expectations for the relationship and communicate your value as a trusted and authoritative confidante.

A **scope letter** is a document that outlines your involvement in a project. It details what you're responsible for, what the customer is responsible for and defines guidelines and boundaries. It may also contain information about the estimated budget, as based on the customer's criteria.

An **enabling agreement** is a document that "locks in" your product or service. The agreement proves hugely beneficial when dealing with multiple influencers who may or may not be voters. The document also sets standards for the project and promises both parties of a mutually coordinated effort.

To use the documents well, you must decide prior to going into a sale if you actually need to mitigate risk, set standards for what other parties will do to reduce risk, and identify how important risk is to the business. You also need to know how much risk your company is willing to mitigate. Some businesses care a great deal about risk, while others don't. You should find out that information during an early fact-finding discussion so that you can tailor your sales proposal accordingly.

Closing Thoughts

If you want to win more sales, you have to go above and beyond the "call of duty". Maybe you've established value or developed relationships with the influencers. Perhaps you hold court as the most knowledgeable person in the room and have won some votes.

However, if your presence doesn't mitigate risk, you could still lose the sale. Your job is to get the buyer past all the hurdles, including risk, so that they choose your product or service. If you can complete that task you will better surround and subsequently close the sale.

CHAPTER SEVEN
Keep the Doors Open with Communication

"The future is too far away."

Building relationships for future sales and business is important, but the future is too far away at times. You need to pay attention to what's in front of you right now to get to tomorrow.

Doing so requires a careful evaluation of daily activities and weeding out the ones that don't lead to success. You can spend all day answering emails and talking on the phone, but if the conversations don't produce sales, there's no point. You need to communicate with your stakeholders and influencers, but you need to do it in a way that guides them ever closer to the assumptive close.

What I'm ultimately talking about is the busy work of communication versus the truly effective communication. The former looks productive, but it doesn't result in sales. In fact, it often leaves you scattered and unable to focus on taking any sale from start to finish. The latter always produces results. It establishes rapport, builds respect and trust, and creates space for honest conversations.

Effective communication is a skill that allows you to understand and better connect with stakeholders and influencers. In sales, effective communication differentiates the good from the great salesperson.

Stakeholders won't share business challenges with someone who railroads them into a purchase or who can't shut up. They will, however, share their concerns with a salesperson who listens and asks questions before proffering a solution.

To help you build effective communication skills, remember the acronym "ART". It stands for **acknowledging** communication's role in close sales, **remembering** that people communicate differently, and **thinking** deep and wide. Those three concepts will be followed by a couple of best practices.

Acknowledging Communication's Role in Closing Sales

Communication in sales involves words, but it might use far fewer words than you expect. Effective communication often occurs when you shut up and listen rather than drone on and on about product offerings and feature sets.

Effective communication also establishes your credibility and expertise. Greg Satell puts the reality aptly in his article, "Why Communication is Today's Most Important Skill."[12]

---

[12] Satell, Greg. "Why Communications is Today's Most Important Skill." February 2015. Accessed January 2016. <https://www.forbes.com/sites/gregsatell/2015/02/06/why-communications-is-todays-most-important-skill/#285dcec23638>.

We tend to treat knowledge and communications as two separate spheres. [...] In truth, we can't really know anything that we can't communicate. To assert that we can possess knowledge, but are unable to designate what it is, is nonsensical.

It's also detrimental to the sale. Communication shows that you know what you are talking about. It demonstrates the product and service with well-crafted words and evidence.

Examples from the Road

I was in Miami recently and was invited to a lunch presentation at an architect's office by one of our new salespeople. She'd done her research and was well prepared with product samples, demo equipment, and food. (Food always brings in people.)

She shared that this architect worked on commercial and residential projects and showed me some projects found on the architect's website. But when I asked the lunch attendees about the projects, they shared that their work was predominately residential — approximately 98 percent. Only two percent, if that, fell under the umbrella of "commercial".

My associate went on undeterred and dove into a presentation about our new commercial products. It was a great presentation, but nobody listened. They played on their phones, looked at the pamphlets and other literature, or sought a break to escape the room. The owner, in fact, did escape. The subject matter of the presentation didn't matter to him, and he wasn't going to waste his time listening to it.

The salesperson was prepared. She'd done her

homework. But she failed to listen and lost a potential sale.

Remember People Communicate Differently than You

We all have biases. We also come from different backgrounds and work in a variety of industries. As a result, we have a way of thinking and talking about projects that no one else does. We all have our jargon, clichés, and acronyms.

Such things can create friction and division between you and a stakeholder. You say one thing, but the stakeholder hears another, and vice versa. To overcome those crossed signals, you must turn yourself into a bridge.

Culture stands as an easy example. The presentation you use in the United States probably won't work in China or South America. You have to adapt your presentation and speaking style to the country's way of thinking, speaking, and behaving. It's hard, and it takes practice, but you can do it.

You stumble across other friction points, too. While a top-level influencer might reside in the same country as a mid-level manager, you need to meet them with different "bridges". The second person could be happy with a footbridge: they need information about price. The first might require a drawbridge: they desire data about quality and care about your company's reputation. To get both of their votes, you must use the bridge that will close the gap and secure the sale.

The buyer journey can also affect your bridge. A stakeholder later along the purchasing path might only need a few words or data points to convince them to vote for your product or service. One found earlier in the chain requires more conversations, information, and demonstrations before casting a vote. It's the same bridge with the same destination, but the steps across it begin at a different stage.

Think Deep and Wide to Completely Surround the Job

A single bridge may not close the sale, especially if your project involves people insight and outside the stakeholder's company. When that happens, you need to think deep and wide and employ different bridges. The destination remains the same, but the way you get there differs.

Thinking deep and wide allowed me to speak with specific influencers and to build bridges. As I did that work, I gained the information needed to secure everyone's votes for my company and its products.

Examples from the Road

While working on a contract for an international airport, I initially called on the engineer. I had a relationship with him already, so I followed up with him about his projections, concerns, and scope for the project.

Next, I contact the lighting designers. They also were people I knew from past projects, and they were working on the airport independently from the engineer. I spoke with them to learn about their expectations, estimates, and timeframes.

I started to compile their information into a cohesive

project plan, aiming to encourage coordination and collaboration between the two. The strategy worked! Because I spent time effectively communicating with the engineer and designers, they started to work closer together.

They also came to view me as an integral part of the project, often deferring to my knowledge, expertise, and experience. Because of that, I was eventually able to approach the architect managing the project and come equipped not only with facts and figures, but also team support.

Practice Your Communication Skills

I don't know that practice makes perfect, but practice does make better. Honing your communication skills takes time and energy. But if you want to get better at surrounding and closing sales, you put in the required work. It's the only foolproof method for getting what you want.

Over the course of my career, I've come to embrace five concepts of effective communication.

1. Take Nothing for Granted

If I've learned anything over the past few decades, it's to take nothing for granted. The sale isn't final until it's signed, sealed, and delivered. The influencer so gung-ho about the product or service at the beginning of the buyer journey can become the most obstinate opponent by the end of it.

And emails and phone calls...It never fails that something seemingly crystal-clear is misunderstood. Other times, a request for information goes unfulfilled – usually for reasons that remain mysteries.

When it comes to communication and sales, be smart. Check your assumptions. Make sure people understood the question and know the deadlines.

The less you take things for granted the more likely it is that you'll close sales. You work hard, stay focused, and confirm that everyone's on the same page. You show up, every day, ready to do the work of surrounding the sale and gaining the assumptive close.

2. Know Everyone's Role

Everyone plays a part in closing the sale, from the person on the ground floor to the one making the final purchasing decision. We've covered many of those people throughout the course of the chapters, but to keep things simple, remember two words: influencers and voters.

Voters can be influencers, but influencers aren't always voters. Both, though, affect your probability of getting a sales order. Influencers can determine whether you get the coveted in-person meeting. They can also sway people to their way of thinking, which either helps or hinders your cause.

Voters stand as a subset of influencers. As such, they hold not only influence but also real power. These are the people who hold positions of authority within the company, sign the checks, or develop growth strategies.

To win all the votes, you must communicate with each influencer and voter on their terms. Use their terminology. Listen to their words, but more than that, listen to their tone of voice and observe their body language. The right words unaccompanied by the right tone and nonverbal cues should sound warning bells in your head. Heed them and take action.

3. Know YOUR Role

That action arises from accurately understanding your part in the sales process. You, as the salesperson, maintain a couple of roles. First, you're a confidante. Stakeholders and influencers share their worries and concerns with you in hopes of hearing a solution.

Second, you play a sort of therapist. You dig for the deep answers. Surface ones do you and the stakeholders no good. The best solution only reveals itself as you ask probing questions.

Third, you are a knowledge center. Controlling the outcome, getting all the votes, and the sale, comes down to who holds the most knowledge. That person should always be you.

Fourth, be a problem-solver and communicator. That is what you do, day in and day out.

4. Communicate to Everyone on Your Team

It's always harder to sell in than sell out. You could convince three stakeholders about the worthiness of your product in the time it takes to convince someone on the marketing team that you need new literature or support materials.

It's a frustrating reality, but don't give up. A study from Marketo and App Data Room[13] reports that alignment

---

[13] Marketo. "Jumpstart Revenue Growth with Sales and Marketing Alignment." 2016. Accessed January 2017. <https"//www.marketo.com/ebooks/jumpstart-revenue-growth-with-sales-

between you and marketing makes a huge impact on sales and overall company growth.

- Organizations improve their close rate by **67%**.
- Companies with closely aligned marketing and sales reduce departmental friction by **108%**.
- They derive over **200%** more value from marketing.

But alignment won't happen by accident. It takes work and dedication. You have to consciously choose to communicate your needs to the marketing team. They have materials that correspond to your stakeholder's specific needs and questions. If you can align yourself with the marketing team, you'll be able to get and share that content that much faster.

5. Listen, Listen, Listen

Great sales come from great listening. In fact, listening should top your list of required skills. You can't give the right answer without knowing the right questions first. You may think you know what the problem is, but do you really? Or did you make assumptions based on the people in the room or the company's history?

No matter how much you know already, and you might know a lot, when you visit with a potential customer, put that knowledge aside. You know nothing.

Spanish explains this concept. If you took Spanish in high school or college, you may remember that "to know" can be translated as "saber" or "conocer". The first word relates to basic facts and data, such as a company's Glassdoor rating, number of employees, or

---

and-marketing-alignment/>.

project budget. The second refers to a more intimate knowledge. It arises from personal interactions. So, you know (saber) a lot, but you still know (conocer) nothing.

Fortunately, you aren't stuck in the land of ignorance. By listening, listening, and listening some more, you will get to know your customer and what they need to solve their pain points. You just have to shut up and listen.

Examples from the Road

Every area and geography I travelled to has very distinct norms and practices that are unique to its area. Things like handing a business card using two hands and dropping your head a little when handing it to a person in Asia, especially Japan and China. Business cards are an extension of the person and are not written on or folded or shoved into a notebook. They are to be laid out on the table, so you can reference to who you are talking to.

Also, in China, where you sit in the room when you enter is very important. The person you have come to talk to will generally sit in the center facing the door with his/her important people to their right and left. It is interesting to see if the financial people are sitting next to the leader or the logistics or manager are sitting closer, it is a little insight on who they feel is important. In the opposite view, in England, it is like the USA, where people sit randomly around the table and everyone talks and states their piece of what is going on.

I spent a lot of time reading books on business norms that are written to give insight, as well as I read a lot of history books on the areas I was expanding the business. People make a lot of decisions based on the way they are brought up and what they are used to. Being a maverick and trying to change how everyone makes decisions, may be a grand gesture, but it also may take a long time, and a lot of time was something I never had. The future was too far away for me. This does not mean that people are not open to new ways and ideas, it is important that they are introduced in a way that is comfortable for them.

Closing Thoughts

Sales aren't magic tricks. They take research, time, and effort. They also require communication – a lot of it. To make your communication more effective, remember the five concepts:

1.   Take Nothing for Granted
2.   Know Everyone's Roles
3.   Know YOUR Role
4.   Communicate to Everyone on Your Team
5.   Listen, Listen, Listen

If you only remember one of the ideas though, make it this one: shut up and listen. Listen to what the buyer has to say and listen when you gain the assumptive close. More words only jeopardize your position, so **SHUT UP AND LISTEN.**

CHAPTER EIGHT

10 Things to Remember

"There's a System. Sales isn't throwing spaghetti against the wall."

Sales is a system, and, like any system, it needs a little oiling now and again. Personally, I keep the system moving with a couple of statements. My sons would call them anecdotes – nuggets of wisdom accumulated over the years, handed down from a parent, peer, or mentor.

Some of the best ones belong to my dad. Others became a part of my sales process when I was just starting out. A few come from mentors and the inventiveness of my own brain (if I do say so myself).

I encourage you to borrow whichever words resonate. Tack them to a wall somewhere or save them to Evernote. Maybe repeat them a few times to get them stuck in your brain.

Then, when a sale becomes difficult, you'll have a resource from which to draw. The words will surface, and you'll know what to do next to rescue the sale from collapse or ruin.

10 Axioms of Sales

"Sayings" seems to be bland, and "proverbs" overreaching, so "axioms" it is. These 10 have seen me through many, many years in sales. Perhaps they will get you through yours, too.

1. Go Sell Something

"Go sell something" stands as one of my go-to-sayings, probably because my dad used to say it. When all else fails, go sell something. Take a positive step forward. Make that phone call, set up a meeting, or take someone to lunch. If you can't manage that, make some cold calls. You can always take a positive action, as long as it relates to selling something.

2. If it gets to Price, You Lose

Never get into a battle about price. If the conversation rabbit holes down to cost, you lost – guaranteed. The question no longer concerns value or solving problems. It revolves around pennies. You always come out the loser in that situation. You either sell on the cheap to get the sale or lost it to the guy who inevitably comes in at a lower price point.

3. Lead from the Front

You can either lead from the front or the back. I recommend the front because it allows for leadership and collaboration with your stakeholders. The second typically results in a lot of prodding and pushing. If you've ever dealt with livestock or a stubborn two-year-old, you know how difficult, painful, and time-consuming that can be.

Leading from the front requires effort, though. You've got to be in the field meeting with customers, courting prospective end users, and appearing at any meeting that requires some influence and elbow grease. As helpful as social media and global connectivity are, nothing replaces meeting people face-to-face and asking for the order.

4. The Devil is in the Details
We talked about the devil and the details in chapter six. To succeed in sales, you need to know the details of the project. You don't have to be the resident expert on them, but you do need to know what they are and who's responsible for them. The information makes you an invaluable resource to the project and the person who owns it.

5. The Future is Too Far Away
One of my early mentors used to say, "Get outta here! The future's too far away. We need sales NOW." He's right. You need sales now, not potential ones on some hazy horizon. While nurturing business connections and relationships for future sales is important, the work should never come at the cost of present opportunities. Pay attention to what's in front of you. Today's chances to surround a sale will get you to tomorrow and the tomorrow after that.

6. This is not a Hobby
I came up with this when asked about my authority on the subject of sales. Sales is not a hobby. This is a career and I have been working at perfecting my craft for 40 plus years.

If you make your livelihood selling products or services, sales isn't a hobby or a game. It's real work that results in very real outcomes like paychecks, commissions, and job security. That means you and I should take sales seriously. Yes, we can have fun with it and poke humor at ourselves, but we should always stay focused on surrounding more sales.

7. You Don't Understand

We talked about this in chapter three. Whenever I hear, "You don't understand," I know I'm on the right track. Either they haven't yet done what I asked them to do, or they misunderstood what I originally asked of them. When I hear those three words, it's my cue to dig deeper and find better answers.

8. Once You Have an Order, Shut Up and Leave

If I've made this statement once, I've said it a hundred times. I'll say it again: "Once you have an order, shut up and leave." I say the words with legitimate cause. Nothing good occurs if you keep talking after the customer commits to the order. Most people possess a deep-seated need to fill silence with words. Don't be one of them! You'll almost always talk yourself out of a sale. Say thank you, shut up, and leave.

9. Money Talks and Bullshit Walks

As salespeople, you and I are judged by sales numbers, not the amount of time given to making sales calls, finalizing closing activities, entertaining stakeholders, and building relationships. Those activities are expected of us. They help us gain the assumptive close. However, they aren't the metric by which we're measured. We're judged by how much we sell.

10. Remember the ABC's

Everyone has an acronym for ABC, like "Always Be

Closing". It works, but I prefer my acronym: "Aggressive, Bold, and Calculating". As a salesperson, you have to be aggressive. Constantly put yourself in a positive position to close a sale by asking questions, getting in front of people, and following up.

You also have to be bold. Take chances, challenge stakeholders, and put yourself in a position – within reason – to "dare" your company to turn down business. Finally, you have to be calculating. Think about how you invest your time and focus on getting the best returns from that time. You play "risk and reward" with every sale. If the reward is low or the risk too high, find some other sale to surround and close.

Closing Thoughts

This was a short chapter, but as someone once said, brevity is the soul of wit. (And as I like to say, multiplying words only gets you into trouble.) I believe you should use as many words as you need to communicate the point. Any more than that belabors the point. Any less, and people don't get it.

We covered 10 axioms of sales in this chapter. Each relates, in some form or shape, to one of the chapters in the book. May they help you surround more sales. And, if you're ever unsure about what to do next, go sell something. The future's too far away.

CHAPTER NINE
Bringing It All Together

"Go Sell Something"

Starting this book might have been one of the hardest things I've ever done, but concluding it proves equally challenging. Perhaps the solution lies in coming full circle: this is not a marketing book. If you're reading this chapter and wondering why you didn't glean any marketing secrets, that's why.

I'm not in marketing. I'm in sales. The activities relate and complement each other, but they remain separate functions. Maybe I have some insight into marketing. I probably do after spending so many years in sales, but it doesn't really matter, as marketing isn't my area of expertise, nor do I want it to be.

Sales is my domain. I like it. It's a puzzle to solve every day. I look at my pipeline and figure out what information, influencer, and communication is missing. Once I identify those gaps, I fill them to surround and close the sale.

For me, that's the challenge – and the joy – in sales. I've gotten plenty of them of the course of my career. But the true challenge and excitement comes from surround those sales. I meet new people, grow my knowledge, and fine-tune my communication skills.

However, I stay focused on the end goal. It's too easy to get caught up in coordinating a sale and miss out on making one. To ensure that I surround and close the job, I use this system. So, to recap:

1. **Sales serves a purpose.** You are important to the lifeblood of the organization. Never forget that your work has a purpose, and so do you. You have to believe that to be successful in sales.

2. **Establish your value.** Always seek to understand how people perceive value – some think in terms of a Porsche while others prefer the Cadillac. If you understand what people value and how that perception shapes their worldview, you'll find it easier to cement your position with them.

3. **Define Your Influencers.** To get all the votes, you start by identifying the influencers, the people with power. To spot them, draw a circle to figure out who has influence and how much.

4. **Control the Decision through Knowledge.** If you want to control the outcome, you have to be the most knowledgeable person in the room. What you don't know might not kill you, but it could kill the opportunity.

5. **Win the Sale by Getting All the Votes.** Defining your value, identifying the influencers, and sharing your knowledge wins, not some of the votes, by all the votes. You want to sweep the "primary" so that there's no doubt about who wins.

6. **Mitigate Risk to Get the Sale.** Even if you get all the votes, you still have to mitigate the risks. Think of mitigation as an insurance policy for you and the stakeholder. It safeguards business decisions and sets expectations.

7. **Keep the Door Open with Communication.** Communication makes the world go around. It also keeps you top of mind and in the mix. Use the available digital tools but never neglect the face-to-face. It's critical to surrounding more sales.

We followed those seven chapters with "things to remember", sayings I've collected over the years. I suggest saving the ones that apply to your current situation. Use them when you're not sure what to do next.

This book also included a couple of exercises, all designed to help you surround the sale. Like the sayings, you should use them when needed. I still employ many of the exercises, and I've been in this business a long, long time.

Finally, get out of here. The future is too far away, and you've got a job to surround.

About the Author

David Odess is currently retired from sales after 45 years. During those years, Odess was a principal in a Manufacturing Representative Agency in the south Florida area, was a Product Manager for a National Electrical Distributor, as well as starting out as a salesman for a local electrical distributor calling on electrical contractors and small industrial accounts. After moving several times for new opportunities, Odess spent the last 23 years working in management for one of the largest lighting control companies in the USA with the responsibilities of identifying, surrounding and closing large projects around the country and market expansion. Along with this responsibility, Odess has lectured and taught classes on how to surround and close commercial and large projects around the world.

He had the opportunity to also be involved in the worldwide expansion of that company which relocated him and his family to London, England for 8 years followed by two years living in Hong Kong. During those 10 years he drove their market expansion by opening up distribution throughout Europe, the Middle East and Asia. He was involved in the late 90's in the expansion of Las Vegas casinos, the huge growth of Dubai and was successful in

Surround the Job

supplying systems during the building growth of major areas of China with the Olympics and Shanghai city growth.

Today he owns his own consulting firm, STJ-CON, LLC, and is working with companies in helping them manage their growth as well as training their sales people to recognize their opportunities for business growth.

He is presently living in Southeast Florida with his wife, Holly, of 42 years and has three sons involved in sales in different manners and four grandchildren.

He can be reached at djo@surroundthejob.com

Made in the USA
Columbia, SC
28 November 2018